I'm a Little Tadpole

By Maria Fleming

♫ Sing to the tune of "I'm a Little Teapot."

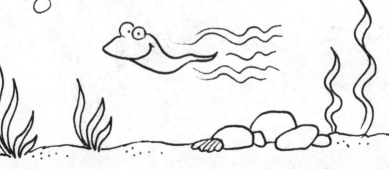

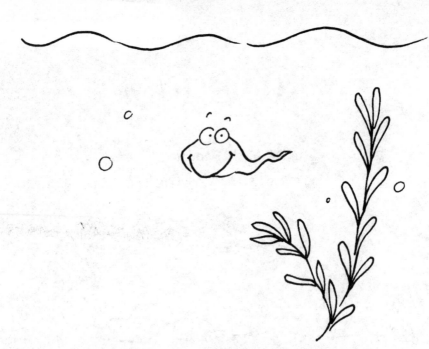

I'm a little tadpole,

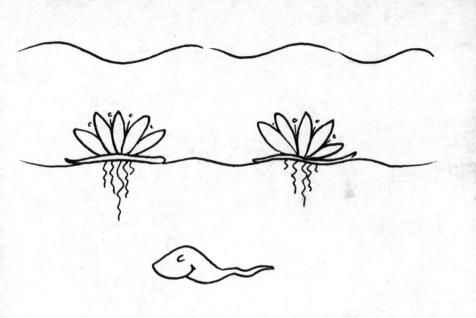

long and thin.

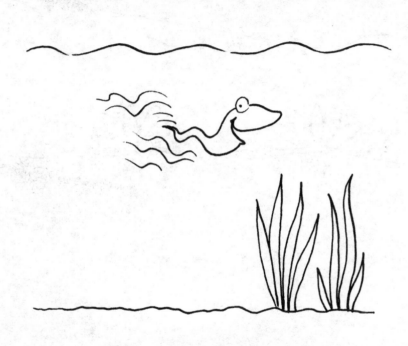

Watch me wiggle.

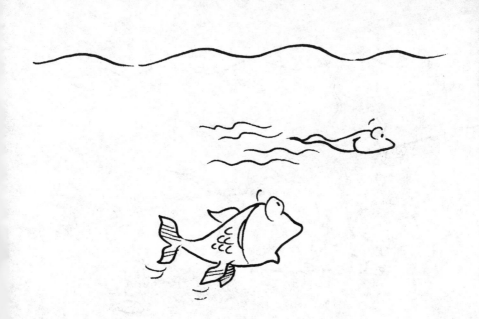

See me swim.

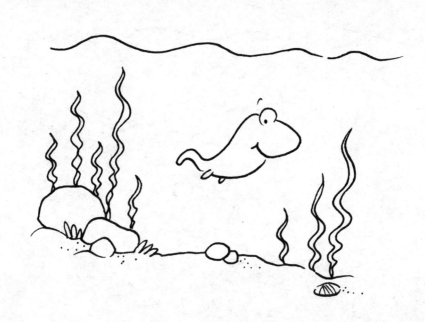

Soon my tail will shrink.

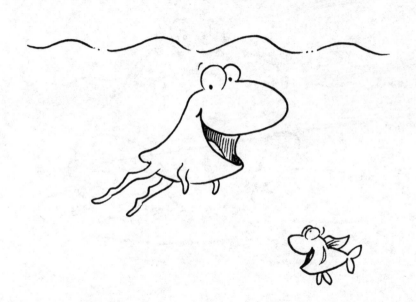

New legs will grow.

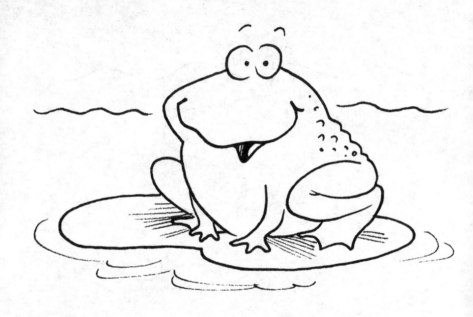

⑧ And I'll be a frog before you know!